INTRODUCTION	3
SHOULD YOU START YOUR OWN BUSINESS?	6
SELF-ASSESSMENT QUESTIONS BEFORE STARTING A BUSINESS:	11
AN EXAMPLE OF WHAT CAN HAPPEN AND HAPPENED TO ME.	14
QUESTIONS TO ASK REGARDING VIABILITY OF YOUR BUSINESS.	15
COMMON TAX BENEFITS FOR BUSINESSES	21
BUSINESS TAX SHELTERS	23
THE STRATEGIC ADVANTAGE OF OUTSOURCING FINANCIAL SERVICES	26
THE GOVERNMENT ROLE IN BUSINESS	31
BRANDING AND MARKETING	36
CREDIT PROFILE FOR YOU AND YOUR COMPANY	40
DIFFERENCE BETWEEN PERSONAL AND BUSINESS CREDIT	41
AVAILABLE LOANS FROM LOCAL BANKS AND LENDING INSTITUTIONS	45

SPECIALIZED LOAN PROGRAMS	47
THE ROLE OF BANKS IN COMMUNITY LENDING	50
LIST OF INFORMATION AND DOCUMENTS BANKS OFTEN REQUIRE.	52
WHAT WE REQUIRE FROM OUR CLIENTS TO HELP THEM GET FUNDING	59
WHAT IS A BUSINESS PLAN?	62
WHAT IS A PROFIT AND LOSS (P&L)?	67
WHAT IS A BALANCE SHEET?	72
WHAT IS A DEBT SCHEDULE?	77
WHAT IS FORECAST AND PROJECTIONS?	82
WHAT IS A CASH FLOW STATEMENT?	86
WHAT IS A PERSONAL FINANCIAL STATEMENT?	91
CONCLUSION	95

Financing Your Vision
Designing a Business Persona for Maximum Funding

Introduction

Before I get into the main topic of this book it is important to give you some context as to the reason for setting yourself up properly whether you are starting your first business or trying to get your existing business to the next level.

Many entrepreneurs get into business because they found something they are good at and want to monetize, and they decide to plunge into the process of running their business. They start selling their products or services and don't always consider the consequences of what it means to own a business. They are mainly thinking about how much money they can earn by selling their products or services.

It is a common theme for many, and I don't blame anyone for wanting to make money and solely thinking about the sales they can make and to whom. However, there are laws and rules that need to be adhere to every where you live. Whether you live in the USA or in another country.

This book is designed to guide you in preparing your company to successfully secure financing or funding. Whether you're launching a startup or managing an established business, numerous essential steps must be taken to ready your company for favorable consideration by local banks or lending institutions.

Whether you're reading this book as someone seeking funding for a newly started business or as someone looking to secure financing for an existing enterprise, the insights provided here will be beneficial to you.

My Experience

I have assisted hundreds of clients in securing funding from banks, and a crucial part of our job is to ensure that these businesses are taken seriously by financial institutions. To achieve this, we often need to restructure their business persona.

For those unfamiliar with the term, a business persona—also known as a brand persona or corporate persona—comprises the qualities, attributes, and characteristics that define a business and set it apart from its competitors. I'll delve deeper into this concept in a later chapter of this book.
The persona of the business owner can greatly influence the business persona, especially in small and medium-sized enterprises where the owner is often integral to both daily operations and strategic decisions. This influence is particularly significant in small businesses, and I will explore this dynamic further in our discussions.

Business sizes range from startups without any funding or experience, operating as one-person entities, to multimillion-dollar companies that have been established for years, employ numerous staff, and have complex funding requirements. Startups, lacking a financial track record, differ significantly from established businesses with proven revenue streams in how they approach funding.

The methods and programs available for securing funding vary widely, and I will briefly touch upon the various forms of financing we've successfully utilized for our clients.

My relationships within the banking sector and other lending institutions have provided me with valuable insights. I've leveraged this knowledge to aid our clients in their quest for funding.

I've also compiled a list of essential information and documents needed to prepare for financing from various sources we've engaged with. It's important to understand that not all funding programs are alike, and not every piece of information will be necessary for each case.

I will present the crucial information for different lending programs. Before we examine that list, it's essential to understand several areas that require attention to organize—or reorganize—your company to ensure it is ready for financing before you submit a loan application.

Expectations

I have compiled several checklists, along with a series of questions and answers, designed to guide you in effectively organizing your startup. For those with established businesses, these resources will aid in reorganizing your company to better position it for funding.

Each section of this book plays a crucial role in properly setting up your company for success. Throughout, you will encounter decisions that need to be made to enhance your company's persona. These are integral steps that you will learn how to navigate as you progress through this book.

Should you start your own business?

The answer to this question varies depending on who you ask. Starting a business is not for everyone, even though I think almost everyone should. There are many benefits of owning your own business. Here are some reasons individuals go into business:

Be Your Own Boss

This is a common motivator. Running your own business allows you to make your own decisions, set your own schedule, and chart your own course. You have the freedom to pursue your vision and build something you can be proud of.

Pursue Your Passion

Many entrepreneurs are driven by a desire to turn their passion into a profession. Starting a business allows you to focus on something you truly care about, and potentially make a living doing what you love.

Financial Independence

While there's no guaranteed path to riches, business ownership offers the potential for significant financial rewards. The success of the business determines your income, unlike a traditional job where salary increases are typically modest and predetermined.

Make a Difference - Impact

Entrepreneurs can create businesses that solve problems, improve lives, or make a positive impact on their community or the environment. Building a business can be a way to address a cause you're passionate about.

Learning and Growth

Running a business is a constant learning experience. You'll be challenged to wear many hats, develop new skills, and adapt to changing circumstances. Entrepreneurship can be a great way to accelerate your personal and professional growth.

Building Something of Your Own

The process of creating and growing a business can be incredibly rewarding. You'll have the satisfaction of building something from the ground up, overcoming challenges, and witnessing the fruits of your labor.

Flexibility and Work-Life Balance

While owning a business can be demanding, it often allows for more flexibility than a traditional job. You might have the freedom to set your own hours and work from a location that suits you, potentially leading to a better work-life balance.

Creativity and Innovation

Entrepreneurship fosters a creative and innovative environment. You'll have the opportunity to develop new ideas, experiment with different approaches, and bring unique solutions to the market.

Personal Satisfaction

The fulfillment that comes from being successful through one's own efforts.

Scale a Product/Service

Taking a product or service that has potential and scaling it up to meet large demand.

Tax Benefits

Leveraging business ownership to take advantage of potential tax benefits not available to employees.

Control Over Workload

Managing their own workload and project choices.

Retirement

Building a business to secure financial comfort for retirement.

Boredom with Current Work

Seeking a new professional path that is more dynamic and interesting.

Utilize Skills and Knowledge

Using their skills and expertise in a way that feels more productive and valued.

Build Wealth

Creating significant asset value that can grow over time, unlike typical salaried jobs.

Create Jobs

Building something that also creates employment for others.

Job Security

Having control over one's own employment instead of relying on the decisions of others.

Leaving a Legacy

Building a successful business can create a lasting legacy. You might create something that endures and provides value to future generations, either through the products or services offered or the impact the business has on the community.

Challenge and Excitement

Owning a business is rarely a smooth ride. There will be challenges, setbacks, and moments of uncertainty. However, for many entrepreneurs, these challenges are what make running a business exciting and stimulating.

Even though there are many good reasons to start a business, you want to ask many questions of yourself to determine if it really is for you and if it will be viable. Here are some questions that you must answer of yourself:

Self-Assessment Questions Before Starting a Business:

Motivation and Passion

Why do I want to start a business?

Is it for financial gain, pursuing a passion, or being your own boss? A strong "why" will fuel your motivation during inevitable challenges.

Am I passionate about the product or service I want to offer?

Passion can help you persevere through difficult times and make sacrifices when needed.

Skills and Experience

Do I have the necessary skills and experience to run a business?

> This includes technical skills related to your product or service, as well as business management skills like marketing, finance, and operations.

Am I willing to learn new skills and adapt to changing circumstances?

> The business landscape is constantly evolving, and entrepreneurs need to be lifelong learners.

Market and Competition

Is there a real need for my product or service?

> Conduct thorough market research to understand customer needs and potential competition.

Who is my target market?

> Clearly define your ideal customer to tailor your marketing and sales strategies effectively.

What is the competitive landscape?

> Analyze your competitors' strengths and weaknesses to identify opportunities for differentiation.

Financial Considerations

How much startup capital do I need?

> Create a realistic budget that factors in all potential costs, including equipment, marketing, inventory, and operational expenses.

What are my funding options?

> Explore various funding avenues such as personal savings, loans, or seeking investors.

Do I have a solid financial plan?

> Develop a financial plan that projects your revenue, expenses, and profitability over time.

Personal Readiness

Am I prepared for the long hours and sacrifices required to start and grow a business?

> Being an entrepreneur requires dedication, resilience, and the ability to handle stress.

Do I have a strong support system in place?

> Having a supportive network of family, friends, or mentors can be invaluable during challenging times.

Once you have answered those questions you will be in a better position to decide if it makes sense for you to run your own business. Now, running the business is not sufficient. You must determine if your idea is a viable one. You want to make certain that the business idea you have is one that is sustainable and will generate the results you are looking to gain.

There is also, the part about your surroundings and any family that you need to contend with. It is not just about the fact that you feel strongly that you can start and run a business and whether it is viable, many of times your circumstances might dictate whether it is the right time to start it or not.

An example of what can happen and happened to me.

I have been an entrepreneur for as long as I can remember. I recall my time during high school when I wanted to be a DJ to make money by throwing parties and being the DJ at my friends' house parties. I don't remember how I got the money, but I went out and purchased two turn tables, a mixer, headphones, a microphone, cables, to interconnect everything, loudspeakers, and a lot of albums and 45's (for those of you who are unfamiliar, these were smaller vinyl records than the albums which were almost twice the size of a 45). I was set to rock and make money in my new venture.

The part I didn't count on is that my parents really didn't like loud music and that they didn't like the idea of me being out late at night.

So, you might have concluded correctly, DJing didn't last long. My parents were the top authority in their home, and I lived in their house, so they decided for me whether it was the right time to start that business.

I laugh about it, now. It was a lesson for me that any business I might want to do, especially while living with my parents needed to be first agreed by them.

When you venture into any business, do take into consideration how it will affect those you count on and those who might impact your surroundings.

Most businesses are started from individuals' homes, and this is when this matters the most. However, if your business will be started outside of your home, then some of these things might not come into play. I do believe that family should always be a consideration as to how and whether you are able to start a business. I indicated the demands of running a business and this can take a toll in anyone's relationship with their loved ones. Keep it in mind.

The steps to evaluate if your idea is a viable business is an important one and should not be overlooked.

Questions to ask regarding viability of your business.

Viability Check for a Specific Business Idea

Conduct thorough market research to validate your idea.

>This involves analyzing market size, growth trends, customer demographics, and competitor landscape.

Talk to potential customers and industry experts.

> Gather feedback on your product or service concept and gain valuable insights.

Develop a business model canvas.

> Define your value proposition, target customers, revenue streams, cost structure, and key resources and partnerships. This tool helps you visualize how all the elements of your business will work together to create value and capture profit.

Develop a minimum viable product (MVP)

> You want to to test your concept with a small group of potential customers. An MVP is a basic version of your product or service that allows you to gather feedback and iterate before making a significant investment.

Competitive Advantage

Identify your unique selling proposition (USP) that differentiates you from competitors.

> What makes your product or service stand out in the market?

Develop a competitive advantage.

> Your competitive advantaged needs to be sustainable in the long term.

Create realistic financial projections.

> You want to do financial projections that forecast your revenue, expenses, and profitability for the next few years. This will help you assess the financial viability of your business and identify potential areas for cost savings or revenue growth.

Research any legal and regulatory requirements.

> It is very important to know requirements that pertain to your business type and industry.

Obtain necessary licenses and permits.

> You want to have all necessary licenses to operate legally and avoid potential problems.

You must remember that starting a business involves risk and uncertainty. By carefully considering these factors and conducting thorough research, you can increase your chances of success.

Business types and formation

> There are minimum documents that most business owners require to start their business. The least we have seen is a business that registered a name at their county clerk's office. Nowadays, however you need a bit more than just being registered as a business in the county your town/city is in. You need to be registered in the state where your business is located and in the federal government (IRS – Internal Revenue Service).

Depending on the state you decide to open your business or have the headquarter for your business the documentation will vary slightly, as well as the cost to form your business also varies, depending on the type of formation you decide to incorporate your business, as well.

This is a topic that can be very lengthy to break down, but I will provide you with a quick overview of the types of business formations that are available.

The IRS recognizes several business structures for tax purposes, but the formation process itself is handled by individual states. Here's a breakdown of the common types:

Structures Recognized by the IRS

Sole Proprietorship

This is the simplest structure, where one person owns and operates the business. All business income and losses pass through to the owner's personal tax return.

Partnership

Two or more people come together to own and operate a business. Profits and losses are shared according to the partnership agreement.

Corporation

A separate legal entity from its owners (shareholders). Corporations pay income tax on their profits, and shareholders may pay taxes again on dividends received. There are two main types:

C Corporation (C Corp)

The default corporation type. Profits are taxed twice (once at the corporate level and again on dividends to shareholders).

S Corporation (S Corp)

A special tax designation that allows profits and losses to pass through to shareholders' personal tax returns, avoiding double taxation.

However, there are stricter regulations for S corporations compared to C corporations.

Limited Liability Company (LLC)

An LLC offers limited liability protection to its owners (members) like a corporation, but with more flexibility in its tax treatment. The IRS allows LLCs to choose how they are taxed:

Disregarded Entity (Single Member LLC)

Treated as part of the owner's tax return, like a sole proprietorship.

Partnership

Treated as a partnership for tax purposes, with profits and losses passed through to members' personal returns.

Corporation

Elect to be taxed as a C corporation.

Formation Process

The process of forming a business is handled at the state level. Each state will have its own specific requirements and filing procedures for each business structure. In general, you'll need to file formation documents with your state's business filing office.

Some business types, like banks and insurance companies, may have limitations on which structures they can operate under.

There are also legal considerations beyond taxes, such as liability protection and management structure, that influence choosing a business formation.

Financial Services Outsourcing

Outsourcing financial roles to a specialized firm can provide valuable insights for business owners on the benefits and necessity of such services for maintaining compliance and optimizing financial operations. This is something you might consider as a first step to review your startup idea and put you in the right path. Businesses that are a bit more established need these services.

Benefits of owning a business

Understanding tax benefits and strategies to legally shelter income from taxes can significantly enhance financial efficiency and profitability. Here are several key tax benefits and business tax shelters that are commonly utilized by businesses to reduce their taxable income:

Common Tax Benefits for Businesses

Business Expense Deductions

Businesses can deduct ordinary and necessary expenses incurred in the operation of the business. This includes rent, utilities, salaries, and cost of goods sold.

Home Office Deduction

For those who use a portion of their home exclusively for business purposes, a portion of home expenses like mortgage interest, insurance, utilities, repairs, and depreciation can be deducted.

Depreciation

This allows businesses to write off the cost of assets over their useful life. It provides a way to recover the cost of substantial assets like buildings, furniture, and equipment.

Vehicle Use Deductions

If a vehicle is used for business, expenses related to its operation can be deductible, either through standard mileage rates or actual expenses like gas, maintenance, and depreciation.

Retirement Plan Contributions

Contributions to retirement plans for employees, including the business owner, can be deductible, providing tax savings while supporting employees' future financial stability.

Tax Credits

Various tax credits are available for specific activities, such as employing individuals from certain groups, investing in research and development, or implementing environmentally friendly improvements.

Section 179 Deduction

Allows businesses to deduct the full purchase price of qualifying equipment or software purchased or financed during the tax year, up to a certain limit.

Carryover Losses

Businesses that experience a net operating loss can carry this loss backward or forward to other tax years, which can offset income and reduce taxes in profitable years.

Business Tax Shelters

Real Estate Investments

Investing in real estate can provide numerous tax benefits, such as deductions for mortgage interest, property taxes, operating expenses, and depreciation. Real estate can also qualify for a 1031 exchange, allowing owners to defer capital gains taxes when properties are sold and the proceeds are reinvested.

Retirement Accounts

Contributions to retirement accounts like SEP IRAs, SIMPLE IRAs, and solo 401(k)s not only prepare for retirement but also reduce taxable income in the year the contributions are made.

Insurance Products

Certain insurance products, such as whole life insurance and annuities, can be used as tax shelters. The cash value growth in these policies is generally tax-deferred.

Charitable Contributions

Donating cash or appreciated assets like stocks to charity can provide significant tax deductions. In the case of appreciated assets, you generally get a deduction for the market value of the asset and avoid capital gains taxes.

Energy Credits

Investments in renewable energy or energy-efficient equipment can qualify for tax credits, directly reducing tax liability rather than just reducing taxable income.

Captive Insurance

Some companies set up their own captive insurance companies to insure against risks. The premiums paid are tax-deductible, and the captive insurance company might benefit from tax advantages if structured correctly.

Municipal Bonds

Although not a direct business operation strategy, investing profits into municipal bonds can provide an income that is often exempt from federal and sometimes state and local taxes.

Strategic Use and Compliance

While these benefits and shelters can reduce tax liabilities, it's crucial for businesses to use them responsibly and in compliance with tax laws. Misusing tax shelters, especially aggressive strategies that may border on tax evasion, can lead to penalties and legal trouble. Always consult with a qualified tax professional or accountant to ensure strategies are implemented correctly and legally. This guidance is vital not only for compliance but also to adapt to changes in tax laws and regulations, maximizing benefits while maintaining ethical standards.

The Strategic Advantage of Outsourcing Financial Services

Understanding the Roles

Accountant

Focuses on the bigger financial picture, offers strategic advice, prepares and reviews financial statements, and assists with business planning and budgeting.

Bookkeeper

Manages day-to-day financial records, ensures accurate recording of transactions, and helps with payroll and invoicing.

Financial Advisor

Provides guidance on financial management strategies, investment decisions, and long-term financial planning to optimize business growth and stability.

Tax Preparer

Ensures compliance with tax laws, prepares, and files business taxes, and advises on tax-saving strategies.

Benefits of Outsourcing

Expertise and Experience

Firms specialize in financial services and bring a wealth of knowledge and expertise that can be costly for a business to develop in-house.

Cost Efficiency

Outsourcing can be more cost-effective than hiring full-time employees, especially when considering the overhead costs of salaries, benefits, and ongoing training.

Scalability

External firms can easily adjust the level of service as the business grows, providing more resources when needed without the complexities of hiring additional staff.

Focus on Core Business Activities

Outsourcing allows business owners to focus on core business activities without being bogged down by complex financial details.

Risk Reduction

Professional firms stay current with regulatory changes and best practices, reducing the risk of errors and ensuring compliance.

Ensuring Compliance

Regulatory Knowledge

Specialized firms are up to date with the latest financial regulations and compliance requirements, crucial for businesses to avoid costly penalties and legal issues.

Accurate Financial Reporting

Maintaining accurate books and financial records is crucial for compliance, especially for publicly traded companies or businesses seeking funding.

Audit Support

Having an experienced firm handle your finances can provide invaluable support during audits by ensuring all financial statements and records are compliant with accounting standards and laws.

Choosing the Right Firm

Assessing Your Needs

Guide readers on how to assess their business's specific needs to find the right type of financial service provider.

Vetting Potential Firms

Tips on what to look for in a firm, including certifications, experience in the industry, client testimonials, and their approach to security and privacy.

Building a Relationship

Importance of maintaining a good working relationship with your financial service provider and how to cultivate that relationship over time.

Outsourcing financial tasks to specialized firms offers several key benefits for businesses, particularly small to medium-sized enterprises and startups:

Expertise and Precision

> Specialized firms bring a high level of expertise and industry knowledge that can be pivotal for maintaining accurate and compliant financial records. Their familiarity with the latest standards and regulations ensures that financial practices meet current legal requirements.

Cost-Effectiveness

> Outsourcing is often more cost-effective than hiring full-time staff, as it eliminates the overhead associated with salaries, benefits, and training. Businesses pay only for the services they need, when they need them, allowing for better control over financial expenditures.

Risk Mitigation

> By employing experts who stay current with regulatory changes and accounting standards, businesses can significantly reduce the risk of non-compliance and associated penalties. These firms also often have robust checks and balances to prevent errors and fraud.

Focus on Core Business Functions

Outsourcing allows business owners and managers to focus on core business activities without being distracted by complex financial management tasks. This can lead to better productivity and faster growth as the management can concentrate on innovation and customer engagement.

Scalability

Financial firms can scale their services to match the growth of a business, providing more extensive support as needed without the business having to hire additional staff or invest in training new employees.

Improved Decision-Making

With access to top-notch financial insights and regular reporting from experienced professionals, business owners can make more informed decisions that are based on accurate financial data.

Audit and Compliance Support

Specialized firms provide invaluable support during audits and other compliance checks, ensuring that the business meets all necessary financial regulations and reporting requirements effectively.

Overall, outsourcing financial tasks to specialized firms can provide businesses with professional, cost-effective, and flexible financial management solutions that support compliance, reduce risks, and allow businesses to concentrate on their primary objectives.

The Government Role in Business

If you are generating revenue the government wants a piece of the money you are generating and once they find out about it they will estimate what you owe and basically send you a bill. In many cases, if you have a location for your business, the local authorities may pay you a visit and ask you for permits, licenses, and other required inspections that might be required depending on your municipality. state, or country.

There are many reasons that we can list for the validity of government getting in your business and of course many reasons why they should stay away and leave us alone to just do the business we want to perform to reach our goals, such as feeding our families, buying that first home or second home, traveling, buying luxury items, or whatever our desires are.

Reasons Government exist at various levels.

Here are some of the reasons governments exist at various levels (municipal, county, state, and national) to address the needs of the people within their jurisdictions. Here's a breakdown of some key reasons for each level:

Municipal Governments

Provide essential services like sanitation, water, and police protection.

Manage local zoning and land use to maintain the character of neighborhoods.

Maintain local infrastructure like roads and parks for residents' use.

County Governments

Coordinate services across multiple municipalities that may be too small to handle them on their own, such as public health or libraries.

Maintain larger infrastructure projects that benefit multiple municipalities, like bridges or regional parks.

State Governments

Ensure basic standards for education, healthcare, and public safety across the state.

Regulate businesses and industries operating within the state.

Build and maintain state-level infrastructure like highways and universities.

National Governments

Provide national defense and security for the entire country.

Conduct foreign policy to represent the country in international relations.

Regulate interstate commerce to ensure fair trade between states.

Issue currency and manage the national economy to promote economic stability.

The truth of the matter is that some government interference may be necessary for many businesses. I will list a few that might resonate with you:

Maintain safety in products and services rendered by each business. Such as in toys for our children and the food we eat.

Maintain safety guidelines in code enforcement to make certain that any structure that is built or installed meets safety requirements, so it won't just collapse on top of us.

Maintain a free market that can be fair to all (even if it is not always the case) it helps that anyone with little resources can start a business.

In local municipalities the need to maintain a similar look and feel is one that maintains uniformity and there aren't all types of structures that don't fit the panorama and the aesthetic.

In import/export the need to maintain price balance around the world.

In the pharmaceutical industry, the need to maintain some type of safety regulations to keep medication for the most part safe. Not a fan of medication, but that is another topic in another book.

As you can see, there are some valid reasons for government to want a piece of your money so it can manage the cost of personnel, buildings, and operations to try and keep us all safe. As they say, everything cost money. I know many of you disagree and there are way too many excesses in government, but it is a necessity to try and have somewhat of a free market. Entrepreneurs thrive in free markets.

Branding and Marketing

Branding and marketing are fundamental aspects of any business operation. They are crucial not only for establishing a presence in the market but also for sustaining long-term growth and building customer loyalty. Below I will discuss the importance of branding, key components of an effective branding strategy, and the role of marketing.

Why Branding is Important

Identity and Recognition

Branding gives your business a unique identity and makes it easily recognizable to customers. This includes visual elements like logos, color schemes, and typography, as well as the business's voice and personality. A strong brand identity helps differentiate your offerings in a crowded market and fosters a sense of familiarity and trust among your customers.

Customer Loyalty and Retention

Effective branding creates emotional connections with consumers, which can lead to enhanced customer loyalty. When customers feel connected to a brand, they are more likely to repeat business and recommend the brand to others. Branding isn't just about attracting new customers; it's also about maintaining ongoing relationships.

Consistency Across Touchpoints

A consistent brand presentation across all platforms and touchpoints increases revenue by reinforcing the brand's message and aesthetic. Consistency helps in building credibility and reliability, which are critical components in fostering trust among prospective and current customers.

Competitive Advantage

A well-established brand can set a business apart from its competitors. By effectively communicating what makes it unique and why its offerings are superior, a business can position itself as a leader in its industry. This differentiation is key to winning over customers from competitors.

Supports Marketing Efforts

Branding supports a business's marketing initiatives by providing a strong base from which to promote its products or services. A clear brand strategy helps ensure that all marketing materials and campaigns are aligned, which amplifies messaging and improves marketing efficiency.

Key Components of Effective Branding

Brand Positioning

This defines how a brand differs from its competitors and where it sits in the marketplace. It involves identifying target markets and tailoring the brand's messaging to meet the needs and desires of that audience.

Brand Voice and Personality

This refers to the consistent tone and personality used in a brand's communications, which should resonate with the target audience and reflect the brand's values and mission.

Visual Identity

Consists of the visual elements that represent the company, such as the logo, color palette, typography, and overall design strategy. These elements should be memorable and reflective of the brand's overall essence.

Brand Experience

Involves all the interactions people have with a brand across various platforms and in the real world. Every touchpoint, from customer service to product quality and marketing materials, should deliver on the brand's promises, contributing to a cohesive brand experience.

Brand Loyalty Programs

These are designed to reward returning customers, encouraging repeat business and fostering a community around the brand. Effective loyalty programs not only increase customer retention but also enhance the overall perception of value within the brand.

The Role of Marketing in Branding

Marketing plays a pivotal role in bringing a brand's identity to the forefront of its target audience's mind through strategic communication efforts. This includes:

Promotional Strategies

Utilizing various channels and methods to communicate the brand's message, including digital marketing, content marketing, advertising, public relations, and social media.

Customer Engagement

Engaging with customers through campaigns, social media, and direct interactions to reinforce the brand experience and gather feedback.

Market Research

Continuously analyzing market trends and customer preferences to refine branding strategies and ensure the brand remains relevant and competitive.

Branding and marketing are not just about getting your target market to choose you over the competition; they are about getting your prospects to see you as the sole provider of a solution to their problem or need. Effective branding elevates a business and builds recognition and loyalty. Marketing disseminates the brand message, creates brand equity, and brings in feedback that informs future strategies. Together, they drive the sustainable growth of the business.

Credit Profile for you and Your Company

The need for good credit goes without saying. We all know that the better our personal credit is the better funding terms and opportunities open for us. Same goes for our company's credit profile.

Importance of Credit

Credit is a cornerstone of financial stability and business development. Both personal and business credit scores serve as crucial indicators to lenders and investors regarding your reliability and financial health. Strong credit can unlock lower interest rates, better loan terms, and higher borrowing limits, all of which are essential for business expansion and managing cash flow. In the personal context, good credit affects your ability to secure mortgages, personal loans, and even impacts insurance rates and employment opportunities.

Overview of the Chapter

This chapter will guide readers through the essentials of understanding, building, and maintaining both personal and business credit. It will cover the definition and measurement of credit, strategies for improving credit scores, and the importance of credit management. Practical advice on leveraging good credit for business growth, along with real-world examples, will equip readers with the knowledge to enhance their financial profile effectively.

Understanding Credit

What is Credit?

Credit refers to the ability to borrow money or access goods or services with the understanding that you'll pay later. **Personal credit** is linked to an individual's financial history and is monitored through personal credit scores. **Business credit** scores, on the other hand, assess the creditworthiness of a business and are crucial for securing business loans and trade agreements.

How Credit is Measured

Credit scores, such as FICO or VantageScore for individuals, and scores from Dun & Bradstreet or Experian for businesses, are quantitative measures of creditworthiness. These scores are influenced by several factors including payment history, credit utilization rate, length of credit history, types of credit used, and recent credit inquiries.

Difference Between Personal and Business Credit

Personal credit is tied to an individual's Social Security Number and primarily tracks perso nal debt and payment history. Business credit scores, which are tied to a business's EIN or DUNS number, focus more on the business's payment history to creditors and suppliers. While personal credit can affect business credit (especially in small businesses), establishing a separate business credit profile is crucial for separating personal liabilities from business operations.

Building Personal Credit

Starting from Scratch

For those new to credit or with a minimal credit history, start by applying for a secured credit card, becoming an authorized user on someone else's card, or taking small personal loans that can be comfortably repaid.

Effective Strategies to Improve Credit Scores

Consistently paying bills on time, maintaining low credit utilization ratios (ideally under 30%), and using a mix of credit types can significantly boost personal credit scores. Avoiding excessive hard inquiries also helps maintain a healthy score.

Monitoring and Managing Your Personal Credit

Regular monitoring of your credit report through platforms like AnnualCreditReport.com, Credit

Karma, or directly from credit bureaus can help you keep track of your credit status and rectify any inaccuracies quickly.

Establishing Business Credit

Creating a Credit Identity for Your Business

Begin by opening a business bank account in your official business name, and setting up a dedicated business phone line to ensure your company is listed in business directories.

Securing Business Credit Lines

Start with a business credit card or a small line of credit from your bank. Use these credits judiciously and make payments on time to build your business's credit history.

Vendor Credit

Utilize trade credits by partnering with suppliers that report payments to business credit bureaus. This not only helps build your credit but also improves cash flow by allowing you to pay for supplies after selling them.

How to Maintain Good Credit

Consistency in Payments

Ensure that both personal and business credit obligations are paid on time. Setting up automated payment systems can help avoid missed payments.

Debt Management

Keep business and personal debt levels in check relative to income and revenue. Utilize financial forecasting to manage debt obligations effectively.

Regular Review and Dispute Resolution

Regularly review credit reports for both personal and business profiles and promptly dispute any errors with the respective credit bureaus to maintain accurate records.

Leveraging Good Credit for Business Growth

Access to Better Financing Options

Strong credit score can provide access to larger loans with more favorable terms, crucial for funding expansion and growth strategies.

Negotiating Power

Good credit provides leverage in negotiations, potentially lowering interest rates and improving loan terms.

Impact on Insurance Premiums and Leasing Terms

Businesses with good credit can benefit from lower insurance premiums and more favorable leasing terms, reducing operational costs.

Available Loans from Local Banks and Lending Institutions

This chapter on the various types of loan programs available for businesses will help you understand your options, the unique benefits of each, and the situations in which they might be most useful.

Traditional Loan Options

Line of Credit

A flexible option where a business is approved for a certain amount of credit and can draw on this line as needed, paying interest only on the amount used. Ideal for managing cash flow and unexpected expenses.

Term Loans

These are loans with a set amount of capital paid back with interest over a predetermined schedule. Good for established businesses looking to finance specific, one-time investments.

Community Bank Lending

Community banks offer a variety of traditional loan products including term loans and lines of credit but stand out due to their local focus and personalized customer service. These banks often have a deeper understanding of local market conditions and a vested interest in local economic development.

Advantages

Personalized Service

Smaller scale operations allow for more personalized customer service and tailored lending solutions.

Local Decision-Making

Loan decisions are made locally, often leading to quicker response times and a greater willingness to negotiate terms based on personal relationships and local economic factors.

Community Support

By working with a community bank, businesses contribute to the local economy, as these banks are known to support local businesses and community projects.

Specialized Loan Programs

SBA Loans

Government-guaranteed loans that offer long repayment terms and low-interest rates. Types include:

7(a) Loan Program

General purpose loans for working capital, expansion, and equipment purchases.

504 Loan Program

Used for purchasing real estate or machinery, offering long-term, fixed-rate financing.

Microloan Program

Smaller loans typically used for startups, offering smaller amounts.

Startup Loans
Loans specifically designed to help new businesses get off the ground. Often requires a solid business plan and good personal credit.

Secured Loans

HELOC (Home Equity Line of Credit)
A personal line of credit secured against the borrower's home, useful for business owners willing to leverage personal assets.

Equipment Financing
Loans specifically for the purchase of equipment where the equipment itself serves as collateral.

Real Estate Loans
Long-term loans used to purchase or renovate business property.

Asset Financing
Loans given against a wide range of business assets including inventory, receivables, or other property.

Alternative Financing

Merchant Cash Advances

An advance paid in a lump sum to a business in exchange for an agreed-upon percentage of future sales. Ideal for businesses with significant sales volume.

Invoice Factoring

Involves selling your invoices at a discount to get immediate cash. Best for businesses that typically wait long periods for payment.

Crowdfunding

Raising small amounts of money from a large number of people, typically via the Internet. Useful for product-oriented startups or businesses looking to test market demand.

Niche Financing

Franchise Financing

Specialized loans designed to help cover the opening costs of a franchise, often provided directly through franchisors.

Microloans

Small loans given to business owners who may not qualify for traditional bank loans, often beneficial for small or startup businesses in underserved communities.

The role of banks in Community Lending

I think it is important to discuss the role of banks when it comes to community lending so you can understand the leverage that small businesses have when working with local banks and the reason it is important and necessary for local banks to work with small businesses. Many think that local banks relax the lending guidelines to small businesses because of a mandate, but it is not a mandate in its face. Here is a quick story as to how community lending came to be.

Community lending by local banks wasn't driven by a single mandate, but rather emerged from a combination of factors:

Local Focus

Historically, banks were local institutions, serving the communities they were physically located in. Loans were made based on relationships and understanding the borrower's situation, not just credit scores.

Regulation

The Glass-Steagall Act of 1933, enacted after the Great Depression, aimed to prevent commercial banks from risky investment activities. This indirectly encouraged community lending by limiting other avenues for banks to deploy their capital. (Note:

Glass-Steagall was repealed in 1999, but community banks continue to play a distinct role.)

Community Needs

Local businesses, especially small ones, often have financing needs that aren't met by rigid criteria of large banks. Community banks fill this gap by understanding the local economy and being more flexible in their lending practices. Government regulators don't explicitly mandate community lending, but they do provide some frameworks that encourage it.

Community Reinvestment Act (CRA)

This 1977 act requires banks to meet the credit needs of all the communities they serve, including low- and moderate-income neighborhoods. Banks are evaluated on their CRA performance during regulatory examinations.

Capital Requirements

Regulatory agencies set capital requirements for banks, essentially the amount of money they need to hold in reserve relative to their loans. This can incentivize community lending, as smaller loans to local borrowers typically carry less risk compared to large loans.

While there's no single requirement for community lending, these factors create a landscape that favors local banks understanding and serving the financial needs of their communities.

List of information and documents banks often require.

Securing funding from local banks and other lending institutions requires careful preparation and organization of various documents and information. This list not only assures the lenders of your credibility and ability to repay the loan, but it also helps them assess the financial health and potential risks associated with your business. Here's a comprehensive list of the information and documents typically required, along with explanations for why they are needed. Do note that not all loan types require all of these documents an information. However, it is a good idea to have them organized and available for those instances where they might be necessary:

Essential Documents and Information for Business Funding

Business Plan

Purpose
> Demonstrates your business's goals, strategies, market, and competitive advantages.

Reason
> Lenders use this to assess the viability and future profitability of your business.

Personal Identification

Purpose
> Valid identification such as a driver's license or passport.

Reason
> Verifies your identity and establishes your legal eligibility to request a loan.

Personal and Business Credit Reports

Purpose
> To assess the creditworthiness of both the business and its principal owners.

Reason
> Indicates the creditworthiness of you and your business, showing how past debts and financial obligations have been managed.

Personal and Business Financial Statements

Purpose

Includes personal financials, business balance sheets, income statements, and cash flow statements.

Reason

Provides a detailed look at the financial status of you and your business, including profitability and cash flow.

Bank Statements

Purpose

Recent bank statements (last 6-12 months).

Reason

Illustrates the business's financial stability and cash management over a recent period.

Tax Returns

Purpose

Recent tax returns (last 2-3 years) for both business and personal.

Reason
> Offers a snapshot of the financial history and is a mandatory check for compliance with tax laws.

Collateral Documentation

Purpose
> Documents that list assets that can be used as collateral.

Reason
> Provides security for the lender; collateral can be seized by the lender to recover losses if the loan is not repaid.

Legal Documents

Purpose
> Business licenses, registrations, franchises, lease agreements, and other legal documents. This includes, Articles of incorporation or organization, and any contracts with significant impact on the business finances.

Reason
> Verifies the legal standing and compliance of the business.

Debt Schedule

Purpose

A comprehensive list of all current debts and obligations.

Reason

Helps lenders understand your current debt commitments to assess additional lending risk.

Ownership and Affiliations

Purpose

To identify the ownership structure and any affiliations that may impact the business.

Reason

Details about owners with significant shares and other companies that may be associated with the business.

Business Insurance Information

Purpose

To demonstrate risk management through adequate insurance coverage.

Details Included

> Policies covering general liability, property, workers' compensation, and potentially professional liability insurance.

Projections and Forecasts

Purpose

> To show the future potential of the business and its capacity for repaying the loan.

Details Included

> Detailed financial forecasts including revenue, expenses, and profitability for the next 3-5 years.

But you might ask yourself, why these documents are needed?

> Banks and lending institutions need these documents to mitigate their risk. By examining these documents, lenders can assess the financial health and operational viability of your business, understand the risk involved in lending to you, and make an informed decision about whether to approve your loan application. These documents show that you are committed to your business and are managing it with a thorough understanding of your financial and operational situation. They also provide essential

information for structuring the loan terms that fit within the risk parameters acceptable to the lender.

What we require from our clients to help them get funding

Let's now get into some of the things that we require our clients to have for us to process a loan for them. We will not proceed with any submission of a loan if our client does not have the required items. If you are going to be serious about getting funding, then you must follow our guidelines to avoid wasting time and making the entire process an efficient one. You don't want to submit any loan request if it is not complete based on the bank's guidelines.

When you submit a loan request, ideally you don't want to have a back and forth with the underwriter regarding missing information or documents. Some loans, like in community lending, usually should not take more than two weeks. Hence the reason we establish a strict guideline with our clients.

If you are submitting a loan for yourself, then you want to make sure that you have all the required documentation and information ready upon submission to the bank.

It is always a good idea to have a good working relationship with your banker. Whether it is the branch manager or the person in charge of submitting the loan request to the underwriters. It goes a long way in making the process smoother.

This list is comprised from our extensive experience with submitting loans to the different local banks. Banks tend to change their underwriting guidelines from time to time. The financial environment changes depending on economic conditions and political landscape, and these forces banking institutions to make changes to their underwriting guidelines.

It is important for you to always ask for the underwriting guidelines for a specific loan type. You want to know what they are looking for in a loan so you can determine if you meet the minimum requirements of that loan program. This is the reason that having a good relationship with local bankers and other lending institutions representatives is so important. They can provide you with information that helps you determine what loan type would be best for you.

The following list applies to what the industry calls NO-DOC loans. These are lines of credit and term loans that require very little documentation, such as the verification of the business being formed with the state and federal government, the verification of the owner and maybe a loan application for some of the banks. Not every institution will require everything that we collect from the client. However, our process is to prepare the client for multiple institutions in case one doesn't fit we try the others.

One of Our Lists

Based on the local banks we have worked with to get our clients a line of credit or a term loan, here is a list of items we need from each client, do note that this list is for no documentation loans and lines of credit, only:

A. Copy of company formation documents (IRS LETTER AND STATE FORMATION DOC) be certain that the company is not revoked with the state. If it is, have your accountant or someone file the annual report. (We sometimes must do this for our client. https://solutionsmsc.com).

B. If the company has a designation of Inc or Corp, or are registered in multiple states, then they will need an operating agreement for the company. (We do draft these for our clients. https://solutionsmsc.com)
C. A copy of driver's license front and back
D. We need an business email address (We can help with it. https://solutionsforsuccess.net)
E. Business phone number (if they don't have one, we can provide them with one. https://solutionsforsuccess.net)
F. They need a website address if it is a type of service business, property management business or a business that communicates information to their clients. (We can get the client the domain, hosting and website, logo design. https://solutionsforsuccess.net)
G. Detailed information on the type of business services and products provided for sale.
H. Mother's maiden name.
I. Copy of social security card, or Passport, or Credit Card.
J. How long at current address, do you own or rent.
K. Name of current business bank
L. Place of birth

I want to provide you with sample of some of the documents banks will need from you when the loan type is more traditional. I will also provide you with the definition of each document.

What is a Business Plan?

A **business plan** is a comprehensive document that outlines the key features of a business, including its goals, strategies, market, financial forecasts, and operational structure. It serves as a roadmap for starting and managing a business, providing detailed plans and projections that are crucial for guiding the business's direction and securing financing.

Purpose of a Business Plan

Guidance and Strategy

It serves as a blueprint for running the business, helping to set objectives, determine the necessary resources, and plan for the future.

Securing Financing

It is essential for obtaining loans or attracting investors, as it shows the viability and profitability potential of the business.

Managing Performance

It acts as a benchmark against which the actual performance can be measured and managed.

Risk Management

Helps identify potential risks and the strategies to mitigate them.

Key Components of a Business Plan

Executive Summary

A concise overview of the business concept, the market opportunity, the unique selling proposition (USP), and a brief summary of financial projections. This section is critical as it needs to capture the interest of potential investors or stakeholders quickly.

Company Description

Provides detailed information about the business, including its legal structure, location, the history of the company, and its mission, vision, and values.

Market Analysis

Demonstrates knowledge of the industry and market. Includes details on market size, expected growth, market trends, and target demographics. Analyzes competitors, their offerings, strengths, and weaknesses.

Organization and Management

Outlines the business's organizational structure, including information about the ownership, management team profiles, and qualifications of the key personnel.

Products or Services

Describes in detail the products or services offered by the business. Explains the benefits, competitive advantages, and the stage of development (for new products).

Marketing and Sales Strategy

Details how the products or services will be marketed and sold. Includes strategies for pricing, advertising, sales processes, and distribution.

Funding Request

If the purpose of the business plan includes securing funding, this section should clearly state the amount of funding needed, the proposed use of funds, and the preferred terms.

Financial Projections

Provides financial forecasts, including projected income statements, balance sheets, cash flow statements, and capital expenditure budgets. For existing businesses, historical financial data should also be included.

Appendices and Exhibits

Includes any additional information that can help establish credibility and trust, such as patents, licenses, leases, and contracts, as well as resumes of key executives, market research data, and relevant images of products.

Importance of a Business Plan

Strategic Focus

Establishes the strategies and objectives for achieving business growth.

Resource Allocation

Provides a framework for decision-making regarding the allocation of resources.

Secure Financing

Essential for communicating with investors and lenders about the business's potential and its funding requirements.

Measuring Success

Helps in setting benchmarks and evaluating performance.

A well-crafted business plan not only guides the company internally but also communicates its value and strategy externally to stakeholders, potential investors, and financial institutions. It is a dynamic document that should be updated regularly to reflect the evolving goals and circumstances of the business.

Sample Business Plan Outline

Here is a basic structure for a business plan:

Executive Summary
- Business Name & Location
- Products/Services Offered
- Mission Statement
- Business Goals & Objectives

Company Description
- Industry Background
- Business Structure
- History
- Unique Selling Proposition

Market Analysis
- Industry Analysis
- Target Market Description
- Competitive Analysis

Organization & Management
- Organizational Structure
- Ownership Details
- Profiles of Management Team

Products or Services
- Detailed Description of Products/Services
- Development Stage
- Pricing Structure

Marketing & Sales Strategy
- Marketing Strategy
- Sales Plan
- Distribution Channels

Financial Projections
- Profit and Loss Statement
- Balance Sheet
- Cash Flow Statement

Debt Schedule
Financial Forecasts and Projections

Appendix
Additional graphs, charts, or documents that support the business plan.

What is a Profit and Loss (P&L)?

A **Profit and Loss statement (P&L),** also known as an income statement, is a financial report that summarizes the revenues, costs, and expenses incurred during a specific period, usually a fiscal quarter or year. This statement provides information about a company's ability to generate profit by increasing revenue, reducing costs, or both. It is one of the three major financial statements used by businesses to track financial performance, alongside the balance sheet and cash flow statement.

Key Components of a Profit and Loss Statement

Revenue (Sales)

This section includes the total income generated from the sale of goods and services before any expenses are deducted. Revenue is often reported as net sales, which accounts for returns or discounts.

Cost of Goods Sold (COGS)

This represents the direct costs attributable to the production of the goods sold by the company. This includes the cost of the materials and labor directly used to create the product.

Gross Profit

Calculated by subtracting COGS from Revenue. Gross profit reflects the profitability of a company's core business activities before overhead costs and other operating expenses.

Operating Expenses

These are the costs related to the operation of the business that are not directly linked to production. Operating expenses include items such as salaries of non-production staff, marketing, rent, utilities, and depreciation.

Operating Income (EBIT)

Stands for earnings before interest and taxes. This is calculated by subtracting operating expenses from the gross profit. It shows the profit generated from regular business operations, disregarding the impact of non-operating activities like interest or taxes.

Other Income/Expenses

This includes revenues and costs not related to primary business operations, such as earnings from investments, foreign exchange gains or losses, and costs of unexpected losses.

Earnings Before Interest and Tax (EBIT)

Also known as operating income, this figure is derived after subtracting operating expenses from gross profit but before the deduction of interest and taxes.

Interest Expense

The cost incurred from any borrowed funds.

Pre-Tax Income

Calculated by subtracting interest expenses from EBIT.

Tax Expense

The income tax owed to federal and state governments for the period.

Net Income (or Net Profit)

The final bottom line figure after all expenses, including taxes, have been subtracted from revenues. It represents the amount of money that the company has either earned or lost during the period.

Importance of a Profit and Loss Statement

Performance Evaluation

Helps stakeholders evaluate the operational performance of the business.

Financial Transparency

Provides clear insights into how revenues are transformed into net income.

Decision Making

Supports management in making strategic decisions based on profitability trends.

Investor and Lender Insights

Essential for investors and lenders as a basis for financing decisions, showing the company's ability to generate profits and manage costs effectively.

Tax Filing

Necessary for accurately reporting business income on tax filings.

The P&L statement is crucial for both internal management and external stakeholders to assess the financial health and operational efficiency of a business. It is also a fundamental tool for budgeting and financial planning, helping businesses forecast future performance based on historical data.

Sample Profit and Loss Statement

Item	Year 1	Year 2	Year 3
Revenue	$150,000	$200,000	$250,000
Cost of Goods Sold	$50,000	$65,000	$80,000
Gross Profit	$100,000	$135,000	$170,000
Operating Expenses			
Rent	$10,000	$10,000	$10,000
Salaries	$30,000	$40,000	$50,000
Marketing	$10,000	$15,000	$20,000

Utilities	$5,000	$5,000	$5,000
Total Expenses	$55,000	$70,000	$85,000
Net Profit	$45,000	$65,000	$85,000

What is a Balance Sheet?

A **balance sheet** is a financial statement that provides a snapshot of a company's financial position at a specific point in time. It details the company's assets, liabilities, and shareholders' equity, helping stakeholders understand what the company owns and owes, as well as the amount invested by shareholders. The balance sheet is one of the core financial statements used in business, alongside the income statement (profit and loss statement) and the cash flow statement.

Key Components of a Balance Sheet

Assets

Assets are resources owned by a company that are expected to bring future economic benefits. They are classified into two categories:

Current Assets

These are assets that are expected to be converted into cash within one year. They include cash and cash equivalents, accounts receivable, inventory, and other short-term investments.

Non-Current Assets (Long-term Assets)

These are assets that provide long-term benefit and are not intended for resale within the year. Non-current assets include property, plant, and equipment (PP&E), long-term investments, intangible assets (like patents and trademarks), and deferred tax assets.

Liabilities

Liabilities are obligations of the company that arise during the course of operations, expected to be settled over time through the transfer of economic benefits including money, goods, or services. Liabilities are also split into two categories.

Current Liabilities

These are obligations due to be settled within one year and include accounts payable, accrued liabilities, short-term debt, and other short-term obligations.

Long-term Liabilities

These are obligations due beyond one year, such as long-term debt, lease obligations, and deferred tax liabilities.

Shareholders' Equity

Also known as owners' equity, shareholders' equity represents the net assets owned by shareholders after all liabilities have been deducted from all assets. It includes:

Capital Stock

The total amount of capital received from investors for shares that have been issued.

Retained Earnings

Cumulative net earnings or profit retained by the company rather than paid out as dividends.

Additional Paid-in Capital

The excess amount paid by shareholders over the par value of the shares.

Treasury Shares

Shares that were once a part of the outstanding shares and were later repurchased by the company.

Balance Sheet Equation

The fundamental equation that represents the structure of the balance sheet is:

$$Assets = Liabilities + Shareholders'\ Equity$$

This equation, known as the accounting equation, must always balance out, reflecting that a company finances its assets by borrowing money (liabilities) or taking from investors (equity).

Importance of a Balance Sheet

Financial Position

Offers a clear picture of the company's financial health at a given moment, showing what it owns versus what it owes.

Credit Analysis and Borrowing

Essential for lenders and investors in assessing the company's capability to handle and repay debt.

Performance Analysis

Helps in assessing operational efficiency, investment potential, and financial strength by comparing various periods and industry benchmarks.

Risk and Return Evaluation

Assists stakeholders in evaluating the risk involved in the company's operations and the potential returns on investment.

The balance sheet is crucial for managerial decision-making, investment analysis, and financial transparency, serving as a basis for computing rates of return and evaluating the company's capital structure.

Sample Balance Sheet

Assets	Amount
Cash	$20,000
Accounts Receivable	$30,000
Inventory	$50,000
Total Current Assets	$100,000
Liabilities	
Accounts Payable	$15,000
Loan Payable	$20,000
Total Liabilities	$35,000
Equity	
Owner's Equity	$65,000
Total Liabilities and Equity	$100,000

What is a Debt Schedule?

A **debt schedule** is a financial document that outlines a company's debt obligations, including details about each debt instrument the company holds. It typically includes information about the amount of debt, interest rate, maturity date, repayment terms, and the schedule for principal and interest payments. By organizing and summarizing the company's debts, a debt schedule provides a clear view of the business's financial commitments and is an essential tool for managing and planning corporate finances.

Components of a Debt Schedule

A typical debt schedule includes the following key elements:

Loan Origination Date: The date when each debt was incurred.
Principal Amount: The original sum borrowed for each debt.
Interest Rate: The rate at which interest accrues on each debt.
Maturity Date: The date by which the debt must be fully repaid.
Repayment Terms: Details on how the debt is to be repaid, including payment intervals (e.g., monthly, quarterly) and whether the payments are interest-only or include principal.
Current Balance: The outstanding balance of each debt.
Collateral: Any assets pledged as security for the debt.

Purpose and Importance of a Debt Schedule

Financial Planning and Analysis

A debt schedule is crucial for financial planning, as it helps businesses forecast cash flow needs based on upcoming debt service requirements. It ensures that sufficient funds are allocated for debt repayment, avoiding potential defaults.

Risk Management

By providing a comprehensive view of all debt obligations, a debt schedule helps businesses manage risk by analyzing their debt load relative to their income and assets. It allows companies to assess their leverage levels and ensure they are not overextended.

Strategic Decision-Making

With a clear understanding of their debt obligations, businesses can make informed strategic decisions, such as whether to refinance debt, invest in new projects, or return capital to shareholders. It helps in evaluating the cost-effectiveness of retiring debt early or restructuring existing debt.

Compliance and Reporting

Debt schedules are important for compliance with loan covenants and other financial regulations. Accurate debt reporting is crucial for maintaining good standing with creditors and investors.

Investor and Lender Relations

A detailed and transparent debt schedule can improve a company's credibility with lenders and investors by demonstrating effective debt management and financial discipline.

Usage in Different Contexts

Corporate Finance

In corporate finance, a debt schedule is used to manage corporate bonds, bank loans, and other forms of corporate debt. It is often part of a larger financial model that projects future financial performance.

Personal Finance

Individuals may use a simplified debt schedule to manage personal loans, credit card debts, mortgages, and other personal financial obligations. It helps in budgeting and financial planning.

Project Finance

In project finance, a debt schedule is critical to ensure that project cash flows are sufficient to cover debt service. It is often used to secure project financing by demonstrating the project's debt servicing ability to potential financiers.

A debt schedule is an essential financial tool that helps businesses and individuals maintain control over their financial health by providing a structured overview of all debt-related obligations.

Sample Debt Schedule

Loan	Origin Date	Amount	Interest Rate	Monthly Payment	Balance
Business Loan	Jan 2021	$50,000	5%	$500	$45,000
Equipment Finance	Mar 2021	$20,000	6%	$200	$18,000

What is Forecast and Projections?

Forecasts and projections are essential components of financial planning and analysis, used by businesses, investors, and financial analysts to predict future financial performance based on current and historical data. While both terms are often used interchangeably, they have specific meanings and purposes in the context of financial management.

Definitions and Differences

Forecast

A forecast refers to an estimate of future financial outcomes that is based on historical data and existing trends. It is usually short-term in nature, covering the next fiscal year or quarter. Forecasts are often updated periodically (such as quarterly or annually) and are used for operational planning and ongoing performance evaluation.

Purpose

The main purpose of a forecast is to provide an informed estimate of what is likely to happen in the near future under current conditions, serving as a practical tool for day-to-day management decisions.

Projection

A projection looks further into the future and involves more speculation, often exploring what could happen under various scenarios. Projections are typically used for strategic planning, considering a range of "what-if" scenarios that reflect different assumptions about the future, such as changes in the market environment, new business strategies, or unexpected economic conditions.

Purpose

Projections are used to model possible outcomes that help businesses prepare for different future scenarios. They are crucial for long-term strategic planning, risk assessment, and investment decisions.

Components

Both financial forecasts and projections typically include several key financial statements.

Income Statement (Profit and Loss)

This shows projected revenues, cost of goods sold, expenses, and net profit or loss over the forecast or projection period.

Balance Sheet

This projects what the business's assets, liabilities, and equity will look like at the end of the forecast or projection period, based on the anticipated business activities.

Cash Flow Statement

This details the expected inflows and outflows of cash, helping businesses understand their future cash position and whether they will generate sufficient cash to meet ongoing operational needs and debt obligations.

Importance in Business

Decision Making

Forecasts and projections provide critical information that helps management make informed business decisions, such as whether to expand operations, invest in new projects, or conserve resources in anticipation of tough economic times.

Financial Planning

They are instrumental in financial planning, helping businesses allocate resources efficiently, manage cash flow, prepare budgets, and plan for capital expenditures.

Risk Management

By examining various possible future scenarios through projections, businesses can identify potential risks and develop strategies to mitigate them.

Funding and Investment

Investors and lenders often require detailed forecasts and projections to assess a company's viability before committing capital. These financial documents provide insights into the company's growth potential and financial health.

Performance Monitoring

Forecasts allow businesses to set performance benchmarks and monitor actual performance against these benchmarks, facilitating timely adjustments in strategies or operations.

Strategic Development

Projections help businesses explore strategic options and prepare for significant changes in their operations or market conditions, supporting long-term strategic planning.

Forecasts and projections are vital tools in the arsenal of any business, enabling better preparedness for the future, optimizing performance and enhancing strategic decision-making. These financial models are crucial for both internal management and external communication with stakeholders.

Sample Forecast and Projections

Yearly Projection for Next 3 Years:

Year	Revenue	Expenses	Net Profit
2024	$300,000	$200,000	$100,000
2025	$350,000	$220,000	$130,000
2026	$400,000	$240,000	$160,000

What is a Cash Flow Statement?

A **Cash Flow Statement** is one of the three fundamental financial statements used to assess a company's performance and financial strength, alongside the Balance Sheet and the Profit and Loss Statement (Income Statement). This statement provides a detailed analysis of what happened to a business's cash during a specific period (such as a month, quarter, or year). It helps stakeholders understand how well the company manages its cash to fund operations, pay debts, and fund investments.

Purpose of the Cash Flow Statement

The primary purpose of the cash flow statement is to provide insights into the liquidity and solvency of a business, showing how it generates and uses cash. It helps stakeholders determine whether a company has enough cash to pay its expenses and purchase assets, or if it might require additional funding.

Components of the Cash Flow Statement

The cash flow statement is divided into three major parts, each reflecting a different category of cash flow.

Cash Flows from Operating Activities

This section measures the cash generated or consumed by regular business operations. It adjusts net income for non-cash transactions and changes in working capital. Common adjustments include:

Depreciation and amortization
Changes in accounts receivable, inventory, and accounts payable
Deferred income taxes
Other non-cash items

Cash Flows from Investing Activities

This section reflects the purchase and sale of long-term investments, property, plant, and equipment, and other business investments. Cash flows from investing activities include:

Proceeds from the sale of fixed assets
Purchases of fixed assets (capital expenditures)
Investments in securities (excluding cash equivalents)

Cash Flows from Financing Activities

This part includes cash flows associated with changes in the company's equity and debt. Typical financing activities involve:

Proceeds from issuing stock
Payments made to repurchase shares
Proceeds from issuing debt (loans and bonds)
Repayments of debt principal (including capital lease obligations)
Payment of dividends

Importance of a Cash Flow Statement

Liquidity Analysis

Helps assess a company's ability to pay off its current liabilities with the cash flows it generates.

Assessing Flexibility

Evaluates a company's ability to take on new ventures or navigate through tough economic times based on available cash.

Performance Metrics

Unlike profits, which can be influenced by non-cash items and accounting methods, cash flow is a more concrete metric of a company's financial health.

Comparative Analysis

Enables an analysis of the difference between net income and net cash provided by operating activities, which can help identify the quality of earnings.

Investor and Creditor Assurance

Provides investors and creditors with clear information about how much actual cash a company has available for items like dividend payments and debt repayment.

Sample Cash Flow Statement Structure

XYZ Corporation

Cash Flow Statement
For the Year Ended December 31, 2023

Cash Flows from Operating Activities:
  Net Income: $150,000
  Adjustments to reconcile net income to net cash provided by operating activities:
    Depreciation: $10,000
    Changes in Accounts Receivable: -$5,000
    Changes in Inventory: -$2,000
    Changes in Accounts Payable: $3,000
  Net Cash Provided by Operating Activities: $156,000

Cash Flows from Investing Activities:
  Purchase of Equipment: -$40,000
  Sale of Marketable Securities: $20,000
  Net Cash Used in Investing Activities: -$20,000

Cash Flows from Financing Activities:
  Proceeds from Issuance of Stock: $25,000
  Payment of Dividends: -$30,000
  Repayment of Bonds Payable: -$10,000
  Net Cash Used in Financing Activities: -$15,000

Net Increase in Cash: $121,000
Cash at Beginning of Period: $50,000
Cash at End of Period: $171,000

This structured overview provides critical insights into the actual cash transactions, ensuring stakeholders understand the liquidity position of the business and its cash management practices.

What is a Personal Financial Statement?

A **personal financial statement** is a document or spreadsheet that provides an overview of an individual's current financial status by detailing their assets and liabilities at a specific point in time. It is essentially a snapshot of one's financial health and is used to calculate net worth, which is the difference between total assets and total liabilities.

Purpose of a Personal Financial Statement

Credit Applications
> Often required by lenders when an individual applies for personal or business loans. It provides lenders with insight into the applicant's financial standing and ability to repay the debt.

Financial Planning
> Helps individuals assess their financial situation, plan for the future, manage budgets, and make informed financial decisions.

Investment Planning

Assists in evaluating investment opportunities and determining risk tolerance based on one's financial capacity.

Estate Planning

Useful in estate planning to ensure assets are distributed as desired upon the individual's passing.

Components of a Personal Financial Statement

Assets

Liquid Assets

These include cash and cash equivalents that can be easily converted into cash, such as bank accounts, money market funds, and certificates of deposit.

Investments

Includes stocks, bonds, mutual funds, retirement accounts, and other securities.

Real Estate

The market value of any real estate owned, such as homes, rental properties, or land.

Personal Property

This covers valuable personal items like vehicles, jewelry, artwork, and collectibles.

Other Assets

Any other assets that do not fall into the above categories, such as ownership interests in businesses.

Liabilities

Current Liabilities

Short-term obligations that are due within a year, such as credit card debts, utility bills, and short-term loans.

Long-term Liabilities

Debts that are due over a period longer than one year, including mortgages, student loans, and other long-term loans.

Net Worth

This is calculated by subtracting total liabilities from total assets. A positive net worth indicates that assets exceed liabilities, while a negative net worth shows that liabilities exceed assets.

Format of a Personal Financial Statement

The format typically includes two main sections: one for assets and one for liabilities, followed by a calculation of net worth:

A personal financial statement provides a snapshot of an individual's personal assets and liabilities, often required by lenders to assess personal credit and financial stability in the context of a business loan.

Sample Personal Financial Statement

Assets	Liabilities
Cash and Cash Equivalents	**Credit Card Balances**
- Checking Accounts: $5,000	- Visa: $3,000
- Savings Accounts: $15,000	**Loans Payable**
Investments	- Car Loan: $10,000
- Stocks and Bonds: $20,000	- Home Mortgage: $120,000
Personal Property	**Total Liabilities**
- Home: $250,000	$133,000
- Automobile: $20,000	
Retirement Accounts	
- 401(k): $50,000	
Total Assets	**Net Worth**
$360,000	$227,000

Conclusion

In this journey through the intricate landscape of entrepreneurship and business ownership, we have uncovered the critical importance of scrutinizing every facet of your business. As we close this guide, it's essential to emphasize that the success of your venture lies not only in your initial vision but in the meticulous attention to the operational, technological, managerial, and financial frameworks you establish.

To thrive in today's competitive market, an entrepreneur must go beyond mere passion. It requires a balanced approach that integrates robust operational strategies, advanced technological adoption, effective management, and sound financial practices. Each component is an ingredient in creating a viable business, where operational efficiencies support technological advancements, management strategies enhance team performance, and financial health ensures sustainable growth.

Remember, the structure you put in place is the skeleton of your business; it supports every move you make and every goal you aim to achieve. Whether you are starting a new venture or refining an established one, the right structure is not just advisable; it is indispensable. It serves as your foundation in turbulent times and your springboard in favorable ones.

As you turn back to your business, equipped with the insights from this book, take a holistic view. Evaluate and re-evaluate not only your business plan but every system and process. The world of entrepreneurship is both challenging and rewarding, and your preparedness to address every aspect of your business will define your path ahead.

Forge ahead with confidence, knowing that the structure you build today will determine the success of your tomorrow.

Let this book serve as your guide, your reminder, and your inspiration as you continue to innovate, manage, and grow. To every entrepreneur who dreams big—keep your vision clear, your strategies dynamic, and your fundamentals strong.

www.ingramcontent.com/pod-product-compliance
Lightning Source LLC
Chambersburg PA
CBHW050233230526
45470CB00005B/1925